COLLECT-A-PET READER

My cute

Pony

Written by Helen Anderton

make
believe
ideas

Reading together

This book is an ideal first reader for your child, combining simple words and sentences with beautiful photography of ponies. Here are some of the many ways you can help your child with early steps in reading.

Encourage your child to:

- Look at and explore the detail in the pictures.
- Sound out the letters in each word.
- Read and repeat each short sentence.

Look at the pictures

Make the most of each page by talking about the pictures and pointing out key words. Here are some questions you can use to discuss each page as you go along:

- Do you like this pony?
- If so, what do you like about it?
- What would it feel like to touch?
- How would you take care of it?

Look at rhymes

Many of the sentences in this book are simple rhymes. Encourage your child to recognize rhyming words. Try asking the following questions:

- What does this word say?
- Can you find a word that rhymes with it?
- Look at the ending of two words that rhyme. Are they spelled the same? For example, "pet" and "yet," or "reins" and "lanes."

Test understanding

It is one thing to understand the meaning of individual words, but you want to make sure your child understands the facts in the text.

- Play "spot the mistake." Read the text as your child looks at the words with you, but make an obvious mistake to see if he or she has understood. Ask your child to correct you and provide the right word.
- After reading the facts, close the book and make up questions to ask your child.
- Ask your child whether a fact is true or false.
- Provide your child with three answers to a question and ask him or her to pick the correct one.

Pony quiz

At the end of the book, there is a simple quiz. Ask the questions and see if your child can remember the right answers from the text. If not, encourage him or her to look up the answers.

Key words

These pages provide practice with very common words used in the context of the book. Read the sentences with your child and encourage him or her to make up more sentences using the key words listed around the border.

Picture dictionary

A picture dictionary page illustrates the things you need when caring for a pony.

Watch me grow

I am a soft and cuddly pet,
but I'm too small to sit on yet!
I need to grow up big and strong,
so you can ride me all day long.

DID YOU KNOW?
Foals usually learn to stand and walk about 30 minutes after they are born.

foal

Time to trot

I love to run! I'm very fast,
so if we race, I won't be last.
Four long legs are all I need
to gallop at my fastest speed!

leg

DID YOU KNOW?
Ponies move at different speeds. Trotting is a slow movement while galloping is very quick!

Big and strong

Now I'm bigger – look at me!
I've grown up strong, as you can see.
I can carry heavy loads
and pull big carts along the roads.

cart

DID YOU KNOW?

Ponies are usually
smaller than horses.

Picking out

I wear big horseshoes on my hooves to keep my feet safe when I move. Clean my hooves out every day to wash the mud and dirt away!

horseshoe

DID YOU KNOW?
It is important to clean your pony's hooves before and after you ride.

hoof

Saddle up!

It feels so nice and warm outside –
the perfect weather for a ride!
Get my saddle and hold the reins,
then we'll explore the fields and lanes.

saddle

DID YOU KNOW?

Riders control their ponies
by pulling on the reins.

rein

13

Grooming

When I've been on a dusty ride,
I'm muddy on my legs and sides.
Groom my coat from time to time
to keep it clean and make it shine.

brush

DID YOU KNOW?
Ponies should not be over-groomed, as this can strip their coats of healthy oils.

Lunchtime

Feed me a meal of grass or hay,
and I will give a happy neigh.
But carrots make a lovely treat –
crunchy, sweet, and good to eat!

hay

carrots

DID YOU KNOW?

Ponies can become overweight if they eat too much grass.

mouth

Whatever the weather

When it feels warm out in the sun,
let's go outside to have some fun.
But we always ride together,
even in cold, rainy weather!

DID YOU KNOW?

Ponies grow thick winter coats to keep them warm during the cold months.

thick coat

Let's go!

It's time to travel to a show –
I hope you know which way to go!
Inside my trailer, I stay dry
while the world goes rushing by.

DID YOU KNOW?

Feeding ponies hay
helps to keep them calm
on a long journey.

trailer

Run and jump!

Show jumping is my favorite thing.
I'll jump over anything:
Big wooden fences, poles, or walls —
as long as they are not too tall!

tail

fence

helmet

ear

DID YOU KNOW?
Jumping is hard for ponies, so they need time to rest afterward.

23

Look at my mane!

I've got a lovely, swishing mane.
It keeps me warm in wind and rain.
Use a brush to keep it neat,
or braid it for a special treat!

DID YOU KNOW?

A pony's mane can be
shampooed and conditioned,
just like human hair!

mane

Zzzzzz

After a ride, I need a rest –
a place that's warm and dry is best.
Leave me somewhere I can nap,
but when I wake up, please come back!

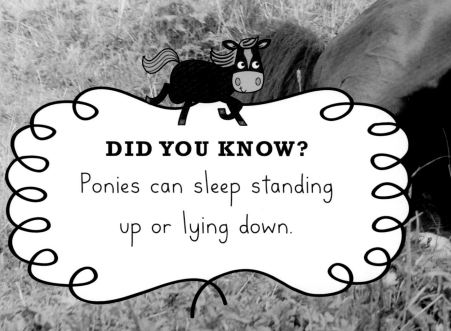

DID YOU KNOW?
Ponies can sleep standing
up or lying down.

Pony quiz

How much do you know about me?

1. Can ponies sleep standing up?

Yes.

2. When should you clean your pony's hooves?

Before and after you ride.

3. Why shouldn't ponies eat too much grass?

It can make them overweight.

4. Are ponies usually smaller than horses?

Yes.

5. How do riders control their ponies?

They control their ponies by pulling on the reins.

6. When do ponies grow thick coats?

During the cold months.

7. Can you wash your pony's mane?

Yes.

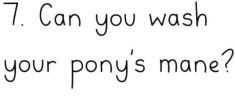

yes ♡ it ♡ see ♡ she ♡ me ♡ of ♡ in ♡ come ♡ will

Key words

Here are some key words used in context. Help your child to use other words from the border in simple sentences.

I **have** a long tail.

I like **to** jump.

on ♡ at ♡ for ♡ a ♡ he ♡ is ♡ go

Look **at** my saddle.

My mane is long.

I eat grass **and** hay.

I **can** sleep standing up.

you ◊ are ◊ this ◊ going ◊ they ◊ away ◊ play

big ♡ have ♡ the ♡ day ♡ get ♡ do

Picture dictionary

brush

cart

fence

hay

horseshoe

reins

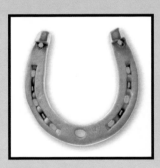

saddle

stable

trailer